REMY KAZENGU MUTOMBO

What Is Wrong With You?

VOLUME 1

king Solomon

Printed and Edited By:

The Motivational Club (Pty) Ltd
2 De Beer Street
Braamfontein
Johannesburg
2001
Republic of South Africa

Tel: +27 (0) 11 046 9394
E-mail: publish@motivationalclub.co.za
Website: www.motivationalclub.co.za

Author's Contacts:

E-mail: kazenguremy@gmail.com

Cell: +27(0) 61 316 7845

ISBN 978-0-620-81456-0

<<<CONTENTS>>>

ACKNOWLEDGEMENTS

My acknowledgement goes Firstly to God the Almighty and Omniscient, the Guide of all researches that have constituted this work.

Secondly, to Jesus-Christ, the Son of God for having given me the opportunity to operate in specifically the apostolic office.
Thirdly to the Holy Spirit for His continuous help throughout the entire process of writing, as well as for opening my understanding of the Bible.

Fourthly, to everyone who contributed in a way or another to the completion of this book, especially to my brother in the Lord Jonathan Ilunga Kabamba for his unending support and supervision.

INTRODUCTION

It is essential to clarify the tittle of the book itself. It is evident that the book will be talking about King Solomon's life, but beyond that He will be used as an example or sample to represent a particular category of people.

King Solomon in this book represents any person who did not have or will not have "Hard work" as the only option that will lead to a successful life. According to the Bible, King Solomon is considered to be the richest and wisest King of his time (1Kings 10:23). Solomon became King in succession to his father David who was a mighty and hardworking man. King David did everything he could to make sure that he who would take over after him may work at ease. Thus King Solomon will be representing any person who was born with everything mostly material things and had everything on a platter of gold to enable them to live a noble life and later succeed in life without having to make so much efforts. Should they be required to make much efforts, they will do so while being already living in much comfort for the simple fact that they would already have had the required wealth and means to live with a peace of mind; does not the Bible Itself say that *money answers everything*? (Ecclesiastes 10:19). Likewise there are people who are born and live in such good conditions; they do not struggle to get money, they just have it.

It will also be important to emphasize that by King Solomon I am not only referring to money that procures a good life, but I am referring to any person who from birth has a particular advantage or strength that no one else possesses, hence be likened to King Solomon, because of that uniqueness they possess, as King Solomon had riches and wisdom that no King in his time had.

Therefore we have some people who are born with a particular physical strength, some other with a particular mental strength and stability, for others it could be intelligence, for others the knowing-how, while others it is the social rank of the family they come from, for others it could be beauty and good appearance, for others it could be a particular talent, for others it could be money; in short something that gives you a certain advantage or edge over others. In fact everyone has something that gives them a particular advantage over others and that spares them from going through certain struggles many will have to go through. As for me, one of my particularities is that God, through Jesus-Christ, found it necessary to give me the ability to be informed in advance about things to happen, even before they take place; a bit like Joseph the son of Jacob in the Bible. And as a result of that I am hardly taken by surprise.

You too have something that God has given you that places you somehow in a position of comfort. All together let go through this journey where we will be discovering mysteries that God has shown me to unveil to His chosen ones.

AIM OF THE BOOK

The aim of this book is to advise "Solomons"; those people if not every one of us possessing particular knowledge, talents, skills, etc. that others do not possess; on how they should conduct themselves. How to utilize that particular advantage they have over others in order to fully fulfill their divine assignment instead of misusing it and ending up very low in life and down on the line. In the introduction to this book it was stated that "everyone has something that gives them a particular advantage over others and that spares them from going through certain struggles, many will have to go through just because they do not possess that particular advantage". However I believe that some people if not everyone will agree with me that people who fail in life are not the most disadvantaged people, but rather people who did not capitalize on their God given strengths, skills, abilities, talents, etc. Therefore in this book I will be referring to all those particularities as potential dangers in the case their possessors misuse them.

MAIN SCRIPTURES USED

The following are the main scriptures used:

- o 2 Samuel 11
- o 2 Samuel 12
- o 1 Kings 1
- o 1 Kings 2
- o 1 Kings 11
- o 1Chronicles22

Chapter One

SOLOMON'S BIRTH

This is how Solomon was born: Once upon a time in 2 Samuel 11:1 as the Bible itself states it *"... in the spring of the year, at the time when Kings go out to battle..."* David being a King also was supposed to go to the battle. However it happened that David did not go, he sent Joab who was the head of his army (2 Samuel 8:16) to the battle. Then it happened as King David did not go to the battle that one evening he woke from his bed and walked on the roof of his palace. As he walked on the roof of his palace he happened to see a beautiful woman by the name of Bathsheba who was bathing. I assume that David saw her naked. David could not resist her and therefore he did all that he could do to end up sleeping with her though she was married to one of his soldiers by the name of Uriah. Sometimes after that act, the woman conceived in her womb and then she sent the news to David the King. When King David received the news, I assume that he was ashamed that the news be spread and hence he made up his mind to come up with strategies that would help him hide the news, so to protect his reputation. David decided to ask Joab the head of the army to send Uriah, Bathsheba's husband, to him so that he would send him back to his house. Actually David's plan was that Uriah would go back to his own house to sleep with his wife in such a way that when Bathsheba pregnancy would become visible; it would appear that she was impregnated by Uriah. However King David's first strategy did not work out as planned due to the fact that Uriah never found it reasonable to leave the others soldiers on the battle field to go back to his own house as though nothing was happening and that everything was well.

So he decided on his turn not to go back to his own house and instead did all that is stated in the same chapter of 2 Samuel 11 from verse 9.

Seeing that his strategy did not work out, King David then thought of a second and final strategy which had for final result killing Uriah his soldier. Thus David sent him back to Joab the head of the army on the battle field as Uriah wished, but this time around David sent him with a letter to Joab informing on the following: " *Set Uriah in the forefront of the hottest battle, and retreat from him, that he may be struck down and die*" (2 Samuel 11:15). So it was and thus Uriah, Bathsheba's husband died. That is what King David did to hide the shame of having impregnated Bathsheba. On her side, when she received the news about the death of her husband, she mourned. And after having mourned, David the King sent and brought her to him to make of her his wife. So she became his wife and she even bore him a son of that pregnancy.

I like our God because He is not a partial God in the way He deals with us human beings as the Bible stated it in Acts 10:34. When one does well, God is pleased with them and when they do evil, God is also displeased with them. That is why you see great servants of God who were once mighty, but who have been reduced to nothing today, because of the wrong they committed. They might have thought that by the works God did through them God was not going to punish them should they do wrong. They might have thought to have become essential to God to an extent which God would not do anything without them.

David too might have thought that he reached the stage where God loved him to such an extent that He would no longer punish him should he act wickedly. He impregnated someone else's wife, he even went further to kill him in order to take the person's wife, and might have thought that God would remain indifferent. However God being impartial, loved David, but was displeased because of the act David committed and therefore punished him.

According to 2 Samuel 11 from verse fifteen, it is recorded that the child was born to David by Bathsheba and died seven day after God struck it with an illness. I consider that this was the *direct punishment* God gave to David for the act of killing Uriah and besides that there was also an *indirect punishment* given to David by God.

Again and again I will always like the way our God deals with us. Before He may even pronounce these punishments to King David by the mouth of Nathan the prophet, God began first to complain over David as He best does it. The Lord complained about David the King in the following words:

"I anointed you King over Israel, and I delivered you from the hand of Saul. I gave you your master's house and your master's wives into your keeping, and gave you the house of Israel and Judah. And if that had been too little, I also would have given you much more! Why have you despised the commandment of the Lord, to do evil in His sight? You have killed Uriah the Hittite with the sword; you have taken his wife to be your wife, and have killed him with the sword of the people of Ammon". (2 Samuel 12:7-9). Likened to how the jury proceeds in court, after God had complained over David, He then pronounced His verdict finding David guilty and therefore sentenced him with the following: firstly, to having the sword not departing from his house and that God would rise up adversity against him from his own house; which I referred to as an *indirect punishment*. Secondly, the sure death of the new born child which I referred to as a *direct punishment*.

The *indirect punishment* is the reason why David suffered adversity for the rest of his life, while the *direct punishment* which resulted in the death of the new born child ended right after the sad death of the child Bathsheba bore with David.

SOLOMON, WHAT IS WRONG WITH YOU?

By that time Bathsheba had already been David's wife, and thus after the sad event, David the King comforted her, then went in to her to lay with her and from that union was born Solomon according to (2 Samuel 12:24).

This is how things had happened before King Solomon came to life. And thus talking about King Solomon without making mention of King David will leave the story incomplete.

<u>What does God teach us through King David's story?</u>

God said to King David ***"for you did it secretly, but I will do this this thing before all Israel, before the sun"*** (2 Samuel 12:12) referring to how David had killed Uriah and took his wife for himself. The lesson we learn from the story is that we do not have to wrong someone many times in order to be punished. Only one evil deed is enough to cause trouble to ourselves. God also said to David that He gave his master's wives into his keeping, which is to say that David had wives and therefore had no reason to do what he did to Uriah. Furthermore God said to him that He would have given him much more should that had been little. I believe that what God wanted to teach David is: "David I, God, have surely given you the power, but the power I, God have given you is not for you to wrong other people even if they are under your authority. I gave you power, however should you desire anything; you ought to ask me instead of you getting it in your own evil way!"

Chapter Two

SOLOMON'S ACCESSION TO THE THRONE

This is how Solomon happened to become the King over Israel after his father David the King was old; many events took place out of which the following will be the focus: According to 1 Kings 1:16-18, Nathan the prophet called Bathsheba, King David's wife and Solomon's mother, to inform her how Adonijah the fourth son of King David had proclaimed himself King over Israel without his father David being aware of that. Thus Nathan the prophet advised Bathsheba that she should go to address the issue to David her husband.

Considering the conversation that took place between Nathan the prophet and Bathsheba the mother of Solomon, I assume that King David had already sworn to her that Solomon her son was the one who would sit on the throne to rule over the people of Israel.

Therefore Bathsheba did so to remind the King of that, lest the King would die without fulfilling that which he swore about, given the fact that Adonijah had already proclaimed himself King, instead of his father. David the King was found in the emergency to do something about the situation, hence He reassured his wife Bathsheba that things were going to happened just as he had already told her.

He said to her: ***"Just as I swore to you by the Lord God of Israel, saying, 'Assuredly Solomon your son shall be King after me, and he shall sit on my throne in my place', so I certainly will do this day"*** (1 Kings1:30). Finally it happened as it was supposed to and Solomon was proclaimed King by David his father.

After Solomon had been made King by his father, the latter gave him charges on how he had to behave. According to 1 Kings 2:1-4, David his father he instructed him to walk in God's ways, to keep His statures, His commandments, His judgments, and His testimonies in order to prosper in all that he was going to do and that God on His turn would fulfill His words that He said to David which words were that David would not lack to have a man on the throne of Israel should he, David, had obeyed to the same charge that he gave on his turn to Solomon his son. Thus David did his work as any good father would toward his son who he's about to carry on with the same work as him.

There is one thing I would like you to understand about the Bible in order for you not to keep incomplete information or to be using biblical verses out of context which is the case on many of preachers nowadays. If you decide to only read the book of Genesis for instance, there will be information that will remain unknown to you unless you read the following books, if not the remaining books. Likewise with the story of Solomon, should you only read the book of 2 Samuel and 1 Kings, there will be information that will remain unknown to you concerning him unless you also go further to read the book of 2 Chronicles. One thing I personally like about the two books of Chronicles is that they give additional information that are very important as these books present information in a chronological order which is actually the reason why they are called Chronicles.

As a matter of fact, the Oxford Advance Learner's Dictionary defines the word chronicle as: "a written record of events in the order in which they happened", that to chronicle something means "to record events in the order in which they happened". Hence the books of Chronicles are entitled so due to the fact that they present events in the order in which they happened.

Moreover, "la Bible de Jérusalem" Bible version in its introduction to the books of Chronicles, Ezra and Nehemiah presents the books of Chronicles as books that give or talk about omitted things which bring a complement to what is already written. Hence it is important to also read the books of Chronicles in order to have much information about King Solomon's story.

Thus concerning King Solomon's story, when reading 1 Chronicles 22, you will discover that though Solomon is the one who built the temple of the Lord, the idea of building it did not come from him, but rather from his father David. Actually David had the idea and all that was required to build that temple. However after God had said to him that Solomon his son was the one who was going to build the temple *" but the word of the Lord came to me… ; 'Behold, a son shall be born to you, who shall be a man of rest; and I will give him rest from all his enemies all around. His name shall be Solomon, for I will give peace and quietness to Israel in his days; He shall build a house for my name"* (1 Chronicles 22:8-10), then David understood that his son Solomon was the one who God chose to build the temple where the Ark of the Covenant would dwell. Thus David; knowing that Solomon was young and inexperienced to carry out that huge task; he resolved to make preparation that his son would need for the construction of that particular temple. Therefore it recorded that David prepared iron in abundance, bronze in abundance beyond measure, cedar trees in abundance.

This was to show that David was the one who knew exactly what was to be built and so he made all the necessary preparations for it, while Solomon on his turn all he had to do was just to put things together. That is why, though the immensity of the work, it is not surprising to read from the Bible that :*" And the temple, when it was being built, was built with stone finished at the quarry, so that no hammer or chisel or any iron tool was heard in the temple while it was being built."* (1 Chronicles 6:7).

David did everything for Solomon his son regarding the construction of the temple to the point where Solomon did not have to worry about anything.

Had Solomon required anything for the construction of that particular temple, according to me, that could have just been an additional thing on top of what his father David had already prepared. In addition to the preparation that David his father had made for him, he also advised Solomon that he was going to need wisdom and understanding from God (1Chronicles22:12). Thus you could read in 1 Kings 3 that when God appeared to Solomon for the first time in a dream of the night to ask him what he would like God to give him that he requested wisdom and understanding. And glory to the Lord our God, who gives us beyond our requests, who gave him not only what he asked for, but in addition to that God gave him largeness of heart as recorded in (1 Kings 4: 29).

Thus King Solomon received from his father advices that he needed to succeed in his life. And so he became the richest and wisest King on the earth in his time to the extent that the entire earth sought of his presence to hear his wisdom (1 Kings 10:23-24; 2 Chronicles 9:22-23). So it was, Solomon received from his father means and advices that he needed to succeed all the days of his life.

SOLOMON, WHAT IS WRONG WITH YOU?

Chapter Three

WHAT WENT WRONG WITH SOLOMON?

There is one thing I like about how the Bible presents King David and King Solomon regarding the mistake or sin they committed. Some will say that it is just a coincidence while others including me will say that it is with a purpose that the Bible presents that part of their lives as such. This is how the Bible presents it: 2 Samuel 11 talks about the sin David committed by taking Uriah's wife who is Bathsheba Solomon's mother. The following book which is 1 Kings on its chapter 11 as well talks about the sin Solomon committed by loving many foreign women. I believe that these two stories were ordered in such a way that one could easily remember them.

Thus this is how the sin of Solomon is introduced in 1Kings 11:1 *[But King Solomon loved foreign women, as well as the daughter of Pharaoh: women of the Moabites, Ammonites, Edomites, Sidonians, and Hittites." And verse 2: "from the nations of whom the Lord had said to the children of Israel, "You shall not intermarry with them, nor they with you, Surely they will turn away your hearts after their god" Solomon clung to these in love.].* This shows that King Solomon was a very wealthy and wise man who was sought to be seen by the entire earth due to what God had given him and who God had made him. However, all that which he had become was ended because of the sin he committed by loving foreign women from the nations of the people God had forbidden the children of Israel to have intermarriages with.

When you read the Bible from Genesis, you will discover that this instruction of not intermarrying with foreign nations was known even by Abraham and the latter transferred that instruction to his son Isaac who on his turn transferred it to his son Jacob and so it was transferred from one generation to the other. Abraham himself was married to Sarah who happened to even have been his relative (Genesis 20:12). This is to show that she was not foreign to him. Thus when Isaac's turn to get married had come, Abraham sent his oldest servant Eliezer to a specific place to find a wife for his son. In order to give his servant a clue on the place where he had to go, Abraham addressed him in the following terms: "but you shall go to my country and to my family, and take a wife for my son Isaac". (Genesis 24:4). The same scenario was noted when Isaac after he had blessed Jacob that he said to him: *["You shall not take a wife from the daughters of Canaan." "Arise, go to Padan Aram, to the house of Bethuel your mother's father; and take yourself a wife from there of the daughters of Laban your mother's brother."]* (Genesis 28:1-2). Actually what Isaac did was to send Jacob exactly where his father Abraham had sent his servant Eliezer to get Rebekah, Isaac's wife. And one thing we noted is that Eliezer prayed to God on his way to the place Abraham had directed him that He would give him success. Therefore I believe that when Isaac sent Jacob to that same place where Eliezer had gone, he knew that at that place Jacob his son was going to succeed. Thus he did not even see the need to pray anymore because a prayer had been made already by the first person who went there.

Thanks to the God of our fathers! They prayed and hence there are things that we are supposed to receive without necessarily praying for.
One thing I like about God is that He is not a discriminatory God to just forbid you to be in contact with a certain category of people without giving you a reason for not doing so.

When God forbade the children of Israel to intermarry with foreign women, the reason to that was: *"Surely they will turn away your hearts after their gods."* (1Kings 11:2).

However King Solomon, despite knowing the reason, decided nevertheless to go after those types of women. Maybe King Solomon trusted and relied on his wisdom without knowing that it was only a matter of time, before he found himself worshipping their gods. From this fact we can understand that whenever God forbids us about something, He knows why and sometimes He will not find it necessary to inform us about the reason, lest we discriminates. One day a servant of God said to me "trust God more than you trust yourself, if God says to you do not go to this woman, trust Him more than you would trust in your own ability to resist". Do not go there and try to resist, just be safe and do not go! So King Solomon might have resolved to trust in his wisdom, than trusting in God and went after those foreign women. In the course of time, King Solomon became old and the foreign wives he had taken turned his heart after their gods to the point his heart was no longer loyal to the Lord his God. It is recorded that King Solomon had seven hundred wives, princesses, and three hundred concubines.

Considering the number of wives and concubines King Solomon had, this shows that it was pretty easy to turn him away from the Lord his God, with his wisdom notwithstanding, and mostly given the fact that he had become old. And secondly it shows that once he had turned away from the Lord his God, it is evident that he was not going to return easily. Thus because he had turned away from the Lord his God; God was angry with him and said to him that: **"Because *you have done this, and have not kept My covenant and My statures, which I have commanded you, I will surely tear the kingdom away from you and give it to your servant."*** (1 Kings 11: 11).

Nevertheless God being a merciful and remembering God, He was not pleased to tear the kingdom away from Solomon while he was still alive, but for the sake of his father David, He decided to proceed in doing so in the days of Solomon's son Rehoboam. Although God resolved to tear the kingdom away from Solomon in the days of Rehoboam, He yet found it pleasing to remember David His servant for having kept His ways, and Jerusalem the city He had chosen in such a way that He planned to give Rehoboam David's grandson to rule as a king over the tribe of Judah which tribe David came from (1 Kings 11:12-13).

In order to accomplish that which He resolved to do after Solomon's heart had turned away from Him, God raised up an adversary against him by the name of Hadad and Rezon (1 Kings 11:14-25). Thus Solomon was no longer a man of rest as God said to David concerning Solomon, but instead Solomon was then seeking to kill his servant Jeroboam, the man God chose to set over the throne of David instead of Solomon because Solomon had sinned against God. Hence Solomon, who was the wisest King of all times, had then to prepare his departure from this earth bearing in mind that a disaster which had never happened to the kingdom of Israel from the time of King Saul up to his own time would happen and his wisdom was going to be powerless about it.

Therefore I am convinced that at that point in time Solomon had understood that it was not his wisdom that had made him become who he was, but that it was the fear of God that lifted him high.

CHAPTER FOUR

WHAT DO WE LEARN?

From this story we learn many things out of which we could talk about the following:

From David's affair with Uriah's wife

1. From the act of killing Uriah in order to take his wife, we learn that we should not use the power, authority or position we have in the society to wrong others. There is always this tendency of people in authority to think that their power, authority or position is unlimited to the point that they can give themselves the privilege to do anything they wish to do. When people who have power, authority do wrong or even evil things it is not because they are necessarily wicked people, but it is just that the power and authority they possess often blinds them, leading them to satisfy their ego to the extent of doing even what is evil. Thus it is important to be led by the Spirit of God. David as a king had the right as a king to get any woman he wished for; however he did not have the right to do so with other people's wives. He took Abigail who had been Nabal's wife as his wife after Nabal died, but the Lord never blamed or punished him because of that for the simple reason that Nabal had already died leaving Abigail as a widow (1 Samuel 25:39-42), but concerning Bathsheba Solomon's mother, David first inquired about her and though he discovered that she was his soldier's wife, David still went ahead to sleep with her and that she even conceived. Then after having tried without success to cover up that mess, he resolved to kill Uriah.

Thus God was displeased and therefore God punished him with an immediate (*direct*) and continuous (*indirect*) punishment to teach him that he had no right to make use of his power and authority to mistreat people. Today in Africa we have leaders mostly presidents who make use of their power and authority to make their own people miserable; no wonder some of them end up very low while others even die of shameful deaths. **Please do not use your power and authority to mistreat the people around you and mostly when they are at peace with you!**

2. From the same story of David's affair with Uriah's wife, we also learn that if you do not discipline yourself by applying self-control; one of the fruits of the Holy Spirit; when God elevates you, you might end up being the cause of your own fall. No one pushed David to sleep with the woman and mostly given the fact that he knew whose wife she belonged to. Thus because of lack of self-control, David occasioned his own fall. **Please let this not be your portion!**

From God's instruction given to the children of Israel

From the instruction God gave the children of Israel to not involve into intermarriages with foreign people, lest they turn away their hearts after those people's gods, there is one thing that is astonishing about it: some of the foreign nations were the Moabites, Ammonites and Edomites.

However when reading the Bible, firstly we discover that the Moabites and Ammonites were respectively the descendants of Moab and Ben-Ammi and these two men were born from the union between Lot and his two daughters as it is known that Lot's wife because of disobedience turned into a pillar of salt on their way out from Sodom and Gomorrah.

His two daughters considering that he became old and not having a son, resolved to make him drunk in order to sleep with him in such a way to give him an offspring that would preserve his lineage (Genesis 19:24-38). Lot himself was Abraham's nephew, the son of Haran who was Abraham's brother (Genesis 12:5).

Secondly, we discover that the Edomites were the descendants of Edom who was actually Esau, Jacob's twin brother and grandsons to Abraham (Genesis 36:1-9). And should Jacob and Esau be Abraham's grandsons while Abraham Lot's uncle, then Jacob and Esau would be considered as sons or nephews to Lot. Which then will lead to deduce or even confirm that the Moabites, Ammonites, and Edomites were relatives to the children of Israel as far as blood is concerned, due to the fact that they all have Terah as their ancestor.

Nevertheless God still referred to the Moabites, Ammonites and Edomites as foreign nations as compared to the children of Israel. Thus this matter raises a question such as why does God still consider these three particular nations as foreign ones to the children of Israel while they were actually blood related? Then we can only have one answer to that question: God's definition of the word foreign is totally different from the human's definition of the same word.

In order for us to understand what God meant by the word foreign, let us go a bit backwards. God had called Abraham who was still Abram at that time from his country and from his family to a land that He was going to show him saying to him:

"I will make you a great nation; I will bless you And make your name great; And you shall be a blessing" (Genesis12:1-3). Then God later confirmed those words in Genesis 22: 17-18 *["blessing I will bless you, and multiplying I will multiply your descendants as the stars of the heaven and as the sand which is on the seashore; and your descendants shall possess the gate of their enemies. "In your seed all the nations of the earth shall be blessed, because you have obeyed My voice."].*

When Abraham had become old and about to die, he then gave all that he possessed to his son Isaac, including that blessing (promises) he had from God (Genesis 25:5). Thus Isaac on his turn, God revealed Himself to him due to the fact that Abraham had passed on to him that blessing (promises) he had received from God. So God spoke to Isaac in the following terms: *[" Dwell in this land, and I will be with you and bless you; for to you and your descendants I give all these lands, and I will perform the oath which I swore to Abraham your father.";* "And I will make your descendants multiply as the stars of heaven; I will give to your descendants all these lands; and in your seed all the nations of the earth shall be blessed;" "because Abraham obeyed My voice and kept My charge, My commandments, My statutes, and My laws."]* (Genesis 26:1-5). When Isaac on his turn had become old and about to die, he blessed Jacob instead of Esau the first born as that was God's choice (Genesis 27).

And furthermore Isaac blessed Jacob again and passed on to him the blessing (promises) that he had received from his father Abraham: *["May God Almighty bless you, And make you fruitful and multiply you, That you may be an assembly of peoples;" "And give you the blessing of Abraham, To you and your descendants with you, That you may inherit the land In which you are a stranger, Which God gave to Abraham."]* (Genesis 28:3-4). And as we all know, Jacob bore twelve sons who later constituted what we call the twelve tribes of Israel.

Therefore, based on the above information, we can then understand that God considered the Moabites, Ammonites and Edomites, etc... as foreign nations simply because they had no share into the blessing of Abraham. In addition to that, those nations had their gods.

Even the children of Israel themselves had to receive Moses as a person sent to them by the God of Abraham, Isaac and Jacob (Exodus 3:15) in order for them to enjoy this divine plan that God had already started with Abraham otherwise they would have remained slaves. And after they had gone out of Egypt, God gave them the law to observe in such a way that they would not do evil practices they had been exposed to in Egypt as well as among the people they met on their way to the promised land.

By that we should understand that as far as God Is concerned, your relatives are not necessarily one nation with you; they can be your relatives, yet foreigners to you as far as God's divine plan for you is concerned. Jesus-Christ Himself made it clear when he said that whoever does the will of His father in heaven is the one to be His brother, sister and mother (Matthew 12:49-50). Therefore your biological mother, father, brother, sister can still be foreigners to you if you do not share the same spiritual conviction with them. Remember we are spirits who live inside physical bodies. That is why if you are a Christian, but have people around you practicing another religion, then automatically they are foreigners to you, even though they are your blood relatives. Likewise those of the children of Israel who never believed or believe in Jesus-Christ are also foreigners.

Thus I believe that those wives Solomon had, though they were his own wives and own concubines, they were still foreigners to him, due to the fact that they had their own gods. And as a result they ended up turning away his heart from his God to theirs. Beloved, whoever turns you away from following God who is revealed to you through Jesus the Christ, is a foreigner to you.
So please stop despising people from other countries, because you think they are foreigners as by now I have revealed to you God's definition of the word foreign!

From Solomon's shameful end

From King Solomon's shameful end, we could learn the following:

1. Much is required from he or she who has been entrusted with much. Solomon was given much by David his father and by God Himself. And if he had known that all he received was to help him focus on his divine assignment of keeping the kingdom, maybe Solomon would have minded his ways. The Lord God had made sure that there was peace in his time to allow him build the temple; as if God said "If your predecessors made mistakes, you who are building the temple are not allowed to make any mistake. And therefore here is everything you need". However Solomon sinned against God despite everything God had done for him. Beloved the advantage you have is not for you to play around with, but rather for you to fulfill your God given assignment. If Solomon's advantage was wealth, wisdom and understanding, for you it might be beauty, intelligence, know-how, power, etc... so may you please make sure that you utilize it to do what God has assigned you to do.

2. From Solomon's fall, we learn that it was not his wisdom, understanding or even wealth that maintained him where God had highly established him, but it was rather the fear of God that he had which kept him up. And once the fear of God was no longer found in him, his wisdom, understanding and wealth were unable to maintain him up there. Beloved, unless God builds, unless God protects; the builders and protectors are doing a vain work says the Bible (Psalm 127:1). Therefore fearing God will make Him build and protect you as true wisdom and understand begins when you fear God (Job 28:28; Psalm 111:10; Proverbs 1:7).

3. From the way God Himself raised up adversaries against Solomon, we learn that it is impossible for God not to find a way to bring you down if you forsake Him. It is rather much simpler for God to bring up adversaries, all He needs is just to go back into your past and bring up on the surface a file that was apparently closed and forgotten. In Solomon's case, God simply raised Hadad who had previously escaped from Joab's sword (1 Kings 11:14-) and that was enough to disturb Solomon for the rest of his life. Beloved none of us is more powerful than God. God can just go back into your past to bring up something you had done in such way to reduce you to nothing in a twinkle of an eye. If some of your close associates can easily put you to shame by exposing your dirty secrets, how much more our God who is Omniscient? Therefore beloved do not make use of that advantage God has given for useless ends, lest He reduces you to nothing as He did with Solomon, because we all have stained pasts! Remember He is the same yesterday, today and forevermore.

4. From the way Solomon ended in this story, we learn that no one is essential for God. Of course God can pass through you to reach people, but that does not mean God is unable to work without you. Surely Solomon had the inborn ability to be a king given the fact that he was from the tribe of Judah. However God could still put him aside to work with someone else. Actually God is the One who chose Solomon from among David's sons to become king after David, hence God could still easily find someone else to replace Solomon. In fact Solomon was not only replaced, but God even took away the kingdom from him in such a way that God gave to Jeroboam his servant ten tribes out of the twelve tribes of Israel constituting that kingdom. Beloved you are privileged to be used by God the way He uses you, hence don't think that God necessarily needs you to do whatever He is doing through you. God is a self-sufficient God.

David says in Psalm 8:4 *"What is man that You are mindful of him, And the son of man that You visit him?"* just to show that it is a privilege to be appointed by God in that office where you are. Therefore obey and fear God!

5. From Solomon's fall, we learn that when God entrusts you with much, that means you have the key in your hands. And should you mess up, you will close that blessing and no one else will be able to receive it. Solomon closed the door to much wisdom, understanding and wealth by turning away from God and thus after him, no one had ever had the opportunity to reach the level he reached and mostly given the fact that the kingdom was divided into two after him while he had been the wisest king who ever existed; what a paradox!

CONCLUSION

I will conclude by saying:

As Solomon had received wisdom, understanding and wealth, the things that distinguished him from all the kings in his lifetime, if not of all the time, so everyone of us has something unique that God has entrusted them with for a specific assignment that needs to be fulfilled by them.

God had entrusted King Solomon with all that I have just mentioned, assets which gave him an edge over all the kings of those days, if not kings of all time. The same way that gift, intelligence, wisdom, talent, skill, strength, etc. is meant to distinguish you and give you an edge over others. However, God has entrusted you with all that not for you to use it at your own freewill to do whatever you feel like doing, lest God reduces you to a common mortal person.

Therefore, you should know that whatever God has entrusted you with is going to distinguish you from other to even give you an edge over them, but bear in mind that no matter how distinguished you are, make sure not to turn away from God by misusing what He has entrusted you with.

Let the Holy Spirit, in the name of Jesus-Christ, complete this book to help you understand what I could not write. Amen!

RECOMMENDATION

The only recommendation or advice that I have for you is that you should start thinking about all that God has gifted you with whether it be intelligence, wisdom, physical strength, mental strength, beauty, money, connections, spiritual gifts, quick understanding, etc... And then begin to convince yourself that all God has gifted or entrusted you with is in order for you to fulfill the divine assignment God has assigned you to.

BOOKS BY REMY KAZENGU MUTOMBO

- o What is wrong with you King Saul
- o What is wrong with you king Solomon